THE HISTORY OF INDIA

THE HISTORY OF INDIA

Published 2023 by History Brought Alive

FREE BONUS FROM HBA: EBOOK BUNDLE

Greetings!

First of all, thank you for reading our books. As fellow passionate readers of History and Mythology, we aim to create the very best books for our readers.

Now, we invite you to join our VIP list. As a welcome gift, we offer the History & Mythology Ebook Bundle below for free. Plus you can be the first to receive new books and exclusives! Remember it's 100% free to join.

Simply scan the QR code down below to join.

THE
VIKINGS
FREE
DOWNLOAD

CONTENTS

INTRODUCTION

India is a land of stories—of grandeur, bravery, pride, and heritage. It is for this reason that it has been referred to as *Bharata-Varsha,* or the Bharata's land, a beloved king from the Puranic traditions. Those are the cultural roots that this peninsular region grows from.

And yet, Indian history has puzzled scores of historians over the last several years. One of the oldest civilizations on the earth has also proven to be one of the most mysterious. For a long time, this civilization that is the source of a tremendously rich heritage has had quite a fragmented record of its evolution. An interested reader for a long time would find patches of great buzz followed by a lull. And this has been a challenge that historians have been trying to overcome.

When looking at history though, it isn't enough to uncover written records. We also need to pay attention to the mindset of the people who produced those records, the lives they lived, the problems they encountered, their spiritual, philosophical influences, and so on. The point of history is not only uncovering facts but uncovering a life lived by people. And whatever gaps the resources may have on Indian historical facts, we have come to hold an increasingly better understanding of the life that people led in this part of the world.

The amount of progress we have made in the last five decades or so is remarkable. That is not to say we have unearthed some astonishing new evidence that wasn't there before. What we have done though is brought together all kinds of records that were uncovered as well as engaged in interdisciplinary exchange to create an all-around understanding. We have borrowed information from architecture and archeology along with studying inscriptions, written text, and coins. But no matter the sources, historians who bring these sources to life in the form of stories deserve all the praise there is.

As we base this book on these same stories, we hope to pay my tribute to all those who have worked tirelessly to tell us more about this brilliant place. Along with that, with this book, we also wish to produce a more concise, cohesive, and smoother recreation of the growth of the Indian subcontinent through the various ages.

Religious Texts as Historical Sources

One thing people living in any historical age seem to have cared about deeply is religion. And you see this care in the amount of effort they put in compiling their religious texts. Evaluating the validity of these texts might be a difficult proposition. But they do provide us with the tools to understand people's psychological mindset when writing the text. This in turn tells us a lot about their lifestyle. For instance, evaluating the Indian Vedas tells us a lot about the spiritual beliefs of the Hindus at that time and also their rituals.

Samhitas, or the four Vedas—Rig Veda, Sama Veda, Yajur Veda, and Atharva Veda—along with the Brahmanas provide us with valuable insights into the philosophical and spiritual world of the Hindus. Other than that, Upanishads examine the existential nature of the Universe, Smritis are narrated from memory (like Manusmriti, Vishnu Smriti, etc.), the Puranas tell the stories of bravery of different famous kings, and many others provide us with more insight. It needs to be remembered, though, that these are ultimately human creations and may not be what happened but what was perceived or remembered or even imagined, in the case of epics like Mahabharata and Ramayana.

Sometimes, cross-matching with other sources helps build a picture. For example, we also have the Buddhist and the Jain scriptures which may provide just as much valuable information when compared as they would individually, maybe even more.

Despite their proneness to inaccuracy, these certainly cannot be discarded and have provided historians with amazing insights into past civilizations.

An Overview of This Book

This book attempts to look at the history of India in an unfragmented manner, right from the beginning until modern times. Note that the book does not dwell for too long in any of the topics, especially because this is designed to be a beginning reference. Often when people try to absorb too much at once, things stop making sense, especially with history where so many things might be happening at the same time and may be equally important to understand the big picture. The purpose of this book is to help you see the entire picture with as much ease as possible. If you wish to learn more, it might be helpful to keep this book as a reference for understanding the chronology of events coming together and then refer to some more advanced volumes on the desired topic.

Let's begin the journey!

PART 1
ANCIENT INDIA

In this part, we decipher the early Indus civilizations of Harappa and Mohenjo-Daro and their contribution to early Indian history. We also shed light on the bridging period between the ancient and the medieval world, which was dominated by two great dynasties—the Mauryas and the Guptas.

CHAPTER 1
EMERGENCE OF CIVILIZATIONS

There is a story in the Hindu tradition that talks about Manu (regarded as the first man in the Puranas). It talks of the time when Manu is drinking water from a pond and he encounters a fish in his palms when he scoops up water. The fish tells him how scared it is that it will be devoured by the bigger fish and urges him to raise it separately until it becomes bigger. In return, it forewarns Manu of the coming deluge. Manu then built a boat which he entered when the flood drowned everything and the fish steered the boat atop a mountain. So, Manu was saved from the disaster, and with his wife, who appeared out of the ocean water, went on to propagate the human race.

The resemblance of this Puranic myth to Noah's ark may not be a coincidence. Many cultures across the globe have documented a similar catastrophe in their mythology. In the present context, this is important because many historians believe this event to have occurred in 3102 BC after which Manu headed the human race as their first great king.

But keeping the gray blend of history and mythology aside, if we focus solely on facts, we uncover a different story that may be patchy and rough around the edges but can at least be corroborated by solid evidence.

The Evolution Through the Ages

Multiple excavation sites across India leave no doubt that this subcontinent had its own Paleolithic men. Crude tools made of "Quartzite," a specific type of rock, have been discovered in many parts. These men and women are likely to have led the same stone-age life as their counterparts on the other side of the world. They were nomadic tribes moving from one cave to another in constant fear of dangerous wild animals and hunting and gathering food as they went. Sources estimate these were stout, dark, curly-haired people to be of the Negrito race and that they were far removed from any understanding of "civilization."

However, as evolution progressed and the future generations of these men and women stepped into the Neolithic age, things changed to an unrecognizable degree. The Indian Neolithic society seems to have made tremendous progress over their rock-wielding ancestors. These Neolithic people had a great talent for agriculture and animal domestication. The days of a vagrant lifestyle were thus over and the age of settlements had begun. Though they had not yet mastered housing, they showed great signs of human evolution. They still lived in cave-like structures but now their caves were decorated with stories in the form of paintings and engravings. They made pottery, clothes, carpentry, and even buried their dead in tombs known as "dolmens." The aim was no more just survival but community and communication. The Neolithic settlements at Burzahom in Srinagar in Jammu and Kashmir are the largest of the many settlements found across the subcontinent.

Despite the discovery of many sites, the information we have on these is still quite limited and is thus characterized as prehistoric, i.e. lacking in a documented record of events. But these archeological findings are enough to let us know that even before the so-called civilizations came about, these people were quite sophisticated in their lifestyle.

Ushering In a New Age

The transition through the ages was, of course, not a smooth one. But today, there is little to no doubt that these Neolithic people were the ancestors of those that brought in the new-age civilizations. While even these new-age civilizations were massively different from our modern societies, they still had some peculiar aspects which made all the future progress possible. The use of metals turned out to be one of these aspects. The use of copper and iron came to be a significant factor in the ushering of the Indus Valley Civilization.

For a long time, almost until the 1920s, the existence of this civilization was completely unknown to us. What's more is when the mounds of Mohenjo-Daro in Sind were discovered, the discoverers didn't even believe they were from the ancient era. That really suggests that these settlements didn't have fancy architectural structures but rather a city that bustled with trade and culture. The houses may not have been examples of aesthetically engaging architecture, but the planning of these settlements was immaculate, to say the least.

These cities flourished on the banks of the Indus river and thus came to be known as the Indus Valley civilization. The fertile soil made agriculture quite a lucrative activity. Trade flourished and the wealth in these cities grew. But unfortunately, the civilization was not immune to natural calamities and war. Some sources say that a massive flood in 2000 BC ruined the settlements beyond repair and the civilization began to decline, finally disappearing around 1700 BC. On the other hand, some other sources approximate that this civilization was razed to the ground in a war somewhere in the 15th and 14th centuries BCE. And still, others believed the civilization was around as late as 1300 BC. Whatever the cause, this civilization remains one of the boldest highlights in the history of ancient India.

The People

Though the settlements began flourishing at the banks of the river, they eventually covered a lot of ground in present-day India and Pakistan. Harappa and Mohenjo-Daro, now located in Pakistan, and Dholavira and Banawali, located in India, were the biggest of the cities of this remarkable civilization.

It's interesting to note that the race of the people in the Indus civilization remains largely unknown. Multiple theories link these people to Elamo Dravidians, the early Munda tribe, and even to the Vedic Aryans, but each of these theories leaves significant gaps in the big picture. Thus, the current understanding is that people of all races inhabited this civilization, though their genetic roots are yet uncertain.

The Lifestyle

The people in this civilization seem to have lived quite a modern and luxurious life. They seem to have had a busy economic, social, religious, and even political life. Though we have no written record for any of this from this time period, the articles unearthed from these sites provide us with detailed insight into the lifestyle of the people.

People consumed a plant and animal-based diet, with locally grown wheat, meat like hens, lamb, pork, and freshly-caught fish. Cotton was commonly used for clothing. They used jewelry items like bracelets and necklaces which have been excavated. Small wheeled carts were used as children's toys, and copper and bronze vessels and articles were used for cooking. They even domesticated animals like sheep, elephants, camels, and buffaloes.

It seems they were advanced not only in social life but also in weaponry—they had elaborate weaponry made out of metal. Though there were axes, spears, and bows and arrows, there were interestingly no swords in use. Seals were used for trade not only with locations in India but even globally.

The most intriguing part of their lifestyle was the interest they took and the time they invested in artistic activities. Their beautiful pottery made with a pottery wheel was a considerable advancement from the crude stone implements. Since the pottery items were used commonly in households, this form of artistry was quite integrated with the Harappan lifestyle. Not only that, but there were also masons, carpenters, and goldsmiths who found ways to incorporate art into the articles of daily use.

There is one aspect though that stands out. Despite the advancement, as mentioned before, there were no architecturally monolithic structures in this civilization. Many historians have pondered over why this could be. The answer lies in the geographical nature of these sites. As they were situated on the banks of a river, they had quite the scarcity of stone. The material used for building their houses was kiln-burnt bricks. Though making such bricks was technologically remarkable for those times, it still did not provide the structure with the strength that stones do. Thus, rather than building taller structures, the Harappans preferred to spread out their construction.

The planning of these cities has a particularly modern, urban feel to them. The roads were built in the form of grids with the narrower lanes joining the broad main roads at right angles. There were granaries, great baths, and a brilliant sewage system that was connected even to the smaller houses.

When it came to the religious affiliations of the Harappans, evidence has been found to point to the practice of animism or worship of inanimate natural elements like stone, water, wind, rain, etc. In other words, the Harappans did not seem to have many gods that resembled the Hindu gods that were worshipped in later times. However, there was one god and one goddess, the remains of which have been repeatedly found across the sites, which seemed to be quite similar to the Hindu god Shiva and Hindu Goddess Shakti. Nevertheless, historians today agree that the religious practices of the people of this civilization laid the foundation for Hinduism which was to come into existence in the coming centuries.

The Vedic Transition

While the Indus Valley civilization blossomed in its urban and contemporary lifestyle, there was yet another civilization getting stronger up north from the Harappan culture. One would think it would have shared at least some similarities with its neighbors but the remains unearthed from the ruins of these settlements tell quite a different story. These people called themselves the Aryas of the Aryans. These settlements did not have any of the urban, modern features of the Harappan cities.

It was the Aryan civilization that is considered the basis of Hinduism as it came to be known later. The animism decreases and names of deities like Vishnu, Indra, etc. start showing up. This community had a patriarchal nature which was again contradictory to the equal status given to all in the Harappan culture. Moreover, their literary texts known as Vedas proved to be a significant source for understanding Hinduism. Unfortunately, as with a lot of ancient Indian literary sources, historians have had disagreements about when the first of these, Rig Veda, was written, making the chronological sequence of events a tad foggy.

The collectivistic values of the modern Indian culture are the product of the family life practiced in the Aryan settlements. While women were treated well, they held a position secondary to their male counterparts. Though there were castes and classes, several instances have been discovered showing marriages between different classes. It is clear that the wealth distribution was quite hierarchical with upper classes engaging in social and artistic living much more than lower classes.

There is no doubt, however, that these Aryans were fierce warriors with intricate weaponry, strong horses, and great military prowess. The Indus Valley civilizations most likely lacked these skills, which ultimately became their downfall. Remember that Aryans were not a united people. Many times they engaged in feuds with many sub-tribes. The Yadu tribe seems to have been the most powerful.

The importance given to the king or the Rajan and emperor or the Samrat is also significant in the Aryan tribes. These kings would engage in sacrificial rituals so as to please the deities. They also had multiple advisors and were expected to govern their people in a moral and just manner. This laid the perfect foundation for an era of massive empires that the subcontinent was to witness in the coming times.

INDIA

CHAPTER 2
THE MAURYAN GLORY

Ancient India's journey into the phase of empires was not a linear one. The evolution of tiny chiefdoms and kingdoms into integrated conquests took centuries to consolidate. The main aspect that distinguished these kingdoms from the empires was not only the expanse of the land conquered but also its ongoing legacy of it. Though these kingdoms would battle each other and the victor would take the territory of the defeated, these territories were not necessarily permanently annexed to the victor's kingdom. While some tribes may have pledged fealty to a powerful king, no significant territorial consolidation came about until around 600 BC when Mauryas built a new political order altogether.

However, before this happened, several powerful kingdoms flourished. The most important ones were Magadha (South Bihar), Vatsa (around Allahabad, now renamed Prayagraj in Uttar Pradesh), Kosala (Oudh, again around Uttar Pradesh), and Avanti (Malwa, Punjab). The story of the expansion of Magadha is the most captivating. Bimbisara and Ajatashatru could arguably be the most powerful of the rulers of this kingdom. They followed a practice of aggressive expansion through conquests and were the primary reason for the growing strength of the Magadhan state.

Then came the Nandas, and this makes for a fascinating story, again. It is said that the last of the successors of Bimbisara's dynasty was Kakavarnin. He was murdered in cold blood with a dagger stabbed in his throat by his own barber. This barber is said to have had an affair with the queen and thus had the ambition of usurping the throne. This barber was none other than the first of the Nanda rulers and was a stern ruler. This first Nanda was responsible for acquiring many kingdoms under him and is considered to have had a significant influence. His successors, however, could not keep up and it is said that the last Nanda ended up being abhorred by his very own subjects. This led to the unavoidable downfall of the Nanda dynasty, which opened the doors for a leader in the form of Chandragupta Maurya to take up the mantle of the emperor.

The Era of Territorial Consolidation

The Mauryan empire was fueled not only by the vacuum created by the hatred towards the Nanda dynasty but by the rapidly changing landscape of the Macedonian conquests in India. In 323 BC, as Alexander, a powerful king from the Macedonian empire, lay on the deathbed, Chandragupta Maurya made the most of this opportunity.

The Mauryan empire flourished between 321 BC and 185 BC and, for the first time in Indian history, consolidated a majority of the subcontinent. Chandragupta Maurya, with the sharp assistance of his advisory minister Kautilya, also called Chanakya, built a model state. Chanakya is famously known for his literary work Arthashastra which is found to be relevant even in this age and times. Arthashastra was the treatise about the model functioning of leadership, government, power, as well as guidelines for economic matters.

Chandragupta Maurya ruled for around 27 years from 324 BC to 297 BC after which his son Bindusara took over. Things continued to be at their peak as the administration went on smoothly. He ruled for another 25 odd years.

When Bindusara died in 272 BC, his son Ashoka took over by defeating his brother.

Ashoka was a fierce ruler, rather the most powerful ruler yet. He was known for his violently aggressive conquests and built the biggest empire the subcontinent had ever seen. It stretched even beyond the subcontinent and covered parts of present-day Iran. As glorious as his conquests sound, they were equally cruel. Though he is said to have been trained in martial arts and the aspects of ruling the subjects, his cruelty earned him a bad reputation. The series of his blood-thirsty conquests continued far and wide until the Kalinga War which ended in 261 BC.

This war was fought between Ashoka and Raja Anantha Padmanabha to gain control over Kalinga (around present-day Orissa). This was the only sizable kingdom that had not yet become a part of the Mauryan empire, and this sat like a painful thorn in Ashoka's side. With his massive army of 600,000 soldiers, 9,000 war elephants, and 30,000 cavalries, the enemy, of course, stood no chance; nonetheless, they are said to have fought valiantly.

This war is regarded as the deadliest of all wars with a casualty figure of nearly 250,000. After this war, Ashoka is said to have walked on the battleground, and as he looked at the bloodshed, remorse filled him. This proved to be a turning point not only for the king himself but the entire history of India. With this war ended the age-old tradition of conquests started by Bimbisara, thereby paving the path for a period of relative peace in the country for a little over three and a half decades. This peace was also accompanied by massive religious changes which we shall discuss in the next chapter. But for now, it would suffice to say that this king, whose early life seems to be lost to history, eventually changed its course in a previously never-thought-of manner, with "conquests of religion."

Dhammavijaya vs. Digvijaya

For a long time, it was believed that Ashoka had turned into a Buddhist monk. Now, however, we know that isn't true. He remained a ruler who followed the Buddhist teachings of Dhamma that is peace and tolerance. He swore to conquer by spreading these teachings (Dhammavijaya) rather than conquering territories (Digvijaya). This was one of the biggest influences on the Buddhist movement in India.

Siddhartha's Awakening

Buddhism came into existence around the

sixth century BC. It was founded by Siddhartha Gautam also known as Gautam Buddha (meaning the enlightened one). Siddhartha was born in a royal Hindu family in Lumbini (current-day Nepal) in around 623 BC and led quite a protected life. There are disagreements over this date too. It is said that there was a prophecy made at the time of his birth that he would either be a great king or become an ascetic. The legend goes on to talk about how Siddhartha, curious about the world, left the palace and thus became aware of four realities of life that turned his perspective around completely—old age, suffering, death, and ultimate truth. These later became the basis of his teachings.

Buddhism is a religion without deities. It's more a way of life and a set of teachings that guide that way. Buddha went around teaching what he had himself learned from his enlightenment under the Bodhi tree. His followers banded into what came to be known as Sangha. These were groups of his disciples that took on this learning and then went far and wide propagating them further. They lived a simple life, away from attachment to material things.

It has been observed that Buddhism has many principles in common with Hinduism from ancient times. Some theological experts even say that Buddhism is like an off-shoot of Hinduism. But regardless of the commonalities and differences, these teachings began to catch on quickly because of the widespread philosophical changes. As Buddhism had a completely internal focus rather than prescribed external rituals, even people from all socioeconomic classes could partake in it equally. Remember that this was also the time that people were getting tired of constant wars. Thus a religion propagating peace was a perfect fit. And on top of everything it promised them a path to salvation that could be followed in this very life.

Ashoka and His Edicts

In the Mauryan empire, Buddhism had a deep influence. Many families were already practicing Buddhist teachings. When it came to Ashoka, it is clear he converted to Buddhism at some point. But what that point might have been is still unclear. Some believe that it was the bloodshed we spoke of in the last section that led him towards Buddhism. Others have another theory.

Prior to becoming the king, Ashoka had already begun to show the makings of a fierce leader. Thus his father Bindusara sent him to Ujjain as his Governor. Here, Ashoka is said to have fallen in love with the daughter of a merchant, Devi or Vidisha Mahadevi. He never married her but they had two children. This woman is said to have been a Buddhist. The current popular belief is that Ashoka was already a non-practicing Buddhist, taking after his lover when he became king, and thus was heartbroken when he realized how badly he had slaughtered men as well as the Buddhist principles.

After adopting Dhamma in the right sense, he went on to propagate its teachings by engraving it on rocks and pillars. These are known as edicts and were placed throughout the empire. Not only that, he even went on tours himself now and then to spread these teachings and also to understand the pulse of his people. People's welfare was given the highest priority. Along with constructing several hospitals for people and animals, watersheds, rest houses, and other such public welfare projects, he also constructed Stupas and Viharas for the monks.

He even sent his son Mahinda and daughter Sanghamitta to Sri Lanka to spread the teachings of Buddhism. It is because of this that Buddhism seems to have been integrated more and more with the common people's lives.

Beginnings of Jainism

The Mauryans, right from Chandragupta Maurya, had intriguing and vibrant religious beliefs. While Ashoka propagated Buddhism, seeds of Jainism had already been planted by the first great Mauryan, Chandragupta Maurya. It is said that Lord Mahavira, the founder of Jainism, often preached to the Mauryas. While some sources say Chandragupta was born to a high-caste Kshatriya family but later converted to Jainism, there are others that portray him as having been a Jain king right from the beginning. Whatever the case may be, it is clear that Mauryans weren't restricted by closed religious boundaries but, on the contrary, have been seen to adopt other religions openly.

Chandragupta was deeply dedicated to his guru Bhadrabahu, a Jain monk. When the monk decided to move to the south because of an impending famine he predicted, Chandragupta also abdicated his throne and moved to Shravanabelagola with his guru. He remained there until his last days.

Though he himself followed Jainism, he did not propagate it on a great scale. This task was later taken up by Samprati, one of Ashoka's grandsons. He is said to have used Jainism as a shield for gaining back some separated territories by sending soldiers as Jain monks. But apart from this, he seems to have been a great patron of Jainism.

CHAPTER 3

THE AGE OF THE GUPTAS

The Mauryan empire began its downhill journey soon after Ashoka's death in 232 BC. The years that followed have often been considered the Dark Ages of India. For almost five centuries the Indian subcontinent bore witness to several foreign invasions including Bactrian, Parthian, and even Turkestani invasions. No Indian king was now formidable enough to live up to the legacy left behind by Ashoka, and the empire that had Pataliputra (present-day Patna) as its bustling capital eventually receded into complete insignificance.

Though "Dark Ages" may sound sinister, it wasn't all bad. This period saw the expansion of artistic and cultural influences. Under Mauryas, there wasn't necessarily much patronage given for arts. Besides Ashoka's edicts, discussed earlier, there wasn't much in the form of great architectural or artistic structures. After the conquests ended, however, there was a boom in literary, artistic, and scientific advances. Patanjali's text on yoga, Manusmriti (code of law given by Manu), and Vatsyayana's Kamasutra all came into existence in the second century BCE; the first play was written by Ashvaghosha who went on to become the mentee of King Kanishka, yet another powerful king.

The conservative and orthodox mind may consider these advances as secondary to territorial consolidation, but the 400–500 years in between the Mauryas and the Guptas proved to be enlightening. Surprisingly, even Indian rulers engaged in expansion and successfully invaded parts of Central Asia, though not for long. Many kings came and went. The Shungas, Kanvas, Shatavahanas, and the Yavanas (the Indo-Greek invaders) call for a special mention for the campaigns they ran. Their coins and inscriptions provide us with a wealth of information.

The Classical Age

As the age of invasions and experiments passed, the Indian subcontinent finally came into its own with amazing advancements in all fields. The empire flourished between 320 to 550 AD right from parts of southern India, as well as central and northern India. This is known as the classical age especially because of the brilliance achieved in terms of arts, architecture, religion, sciences, and even philosophy. The prosperity and growth attained by the people during this age were particularly remarkable. But interestingly not much is known about the beginnings of this dynasty. However, the travel logs of the Buddhist monks tell us much of what we know.

Another Founder Named Chandragupta

It's a funny coincidence that the course of India's history was changed more than once by a king named Chandragupta, one in 320 BC and the next in 320 AD. Thus, he came to be known as Chandragupta I to avoid confusion. Chandragupta I was not the first of the Gupta rulers but was certainly the first to be recognized for his prowess. The Gupta dynasty seems to have begun with Srigupta, a king of a small kingdom in Magadha and succeeded by his son Ghatotkacha. Chandragupta was Ghatotkacha's son and was indeed the one to take the Gupta empire to never-before-thought-of heights. He was adorned with the title of Maharajadhiraja, or king of kings, as he expanded his small inheritance of a kingdom into a respectable empire either through conquest or by marriage.

It is believed that Chandragupta I was the first of his dynasty to be cast on the seals of the kingdom. Though the expanse of his kingdom is quite large, right from Ganga in Southern Bihar to Allahabad in Uttar Pradesh, not much is known about how he acquired these territories. It is assumed that most of them may have come to him in his marriage alliance with his Licchavi Queen Kumaradevi.

However, no matter the territory expansion, the Guptas still remained an obscure entity in history until the arrival of Chandragupta's son Samudragupta.

Samudragupta and His Conquests

According to an inscription on a pillar found in Allahabad, written in a script known as Ashoka Brahmi, Samudragupta had succeeded his father not only on the throne but was also the rightful successor to his title of Maharajadhiraja (king of kings). He undertook several campaigns that helped him expand the Gupta kingdom. First, he is said to have headed to present-day Uttar Pradesh and Rajasthan and then down south, defeating several more kings. The core of the Gupta kingdom is said to have been around present-day West Bengal, Uttar Pradesh, Bihar, Madhya Pradesh, and parts of Rajasthan and Punjab. Furthermore, several other rulers in and around the Indian subcontinent are mentioned in the inscription to have asked for Samudragupta's help in their own territorial campaigns while accepting his kingdom as a sovereign one itself. In inscriptions, he is often referred to as the world ruler despite his empire being limited to the Indian subcontinent only.

Samudragupta, and rather all the Gupta rulers, seem to have been quite fond of grand titles as well gestures. And thus, these inscriptions need to be taken with a pinch of salt. Samudragupta particularly is said to have performed the Ashvamedha ritual of a horse sacrifice and even gifted 100,000 cows to his Brahmin followers. He is likely to have had a leaning towards the deity Vishnu and has even been characterized as Vishnu reincarnate due to his "world-ruler" fame.

Though nowhere close to, let's say, Ashoka's empire, Samudragupta had amassed a commendable expanse of territory. While the inscription goes on to describe the greatness of this king with several titles, the Gupta kingdom would never be a pan-India empire. This is mainly because of what some historians consider a flawed political policy. It is often surmised that the reason the Gupta rulers did not expand the empire as much as they could have was this very policy.

The Guptas, it has been found, would battle the kings and even win many of those battles. But they hardly ever annexed these territories to their own kingdom. These kingdoms were only asked to pay some kind of a tribute to the Gupta victors after which the defeated kings were allowed to run their kingdoms as before and the Gupta forces withdrew. On the one hand, this helped the Guptas accumulate massive amounts of wealth which would then be used as patronage for different forms of artistic and cultural projects. But on the other hand, it completely undermined the political hold of the Guptas by reducing battles and conquests only to a manner of exchanging wealth. Rather than territorial consolidation. Of course, for what it's worth this may be considered by some just a clever way of amassing wealth apart from violence and brutal aggression, especially as feudalism was becoming stronger.

But regardless of the policy he followed, Samudragupta also maintained a fierce military. It has been observed by many historians that the Guptas were fantastic adaptors and adapted their military equipment as well as battle styles based on the opponents they faced, specifically the

Scythians like Shakas and the Kushanas. Samudragupta is even seen donning a Scythian-inspired costume on his gold coins. The Gupta army had even fashioned camouflage garments made using Bandhani (tie-dye) techniques to be used for tactical advantage.

It must be noted that Samudragupta was not only a great warrior but also a great patron of art and culture. The characteristic classical age is in great parts attributed to his reign and his love for arts. He is said to have been a great musician himself. He has been portrayed as a ruler that gave prime importance to the welfare of his subjects and closely followed the Kautilyan Arthashastra guidelines for running the model state. It may well be said that it was Samudragupta who created a prototype that exhibited a strategy that indeed changed the manner of administration and battle for the coming generations.

Samudragupta was succeeded by Chandragupta II also known as Vikramaditya. It is said that he, Chandragupta II, deposed his older brother Ramagupta and attained the right to the throne. Chandragupta II also followed in his father's footsteps, maintaining the empire created by his father and following the same policies.

Life in the Gupta Empire

Since the Gupta rule has been rightly termed

as the “golden age,” it would warrant a closer look at the lifestyle led by common people. It appears that even though these were “happy times” there was still a strong economic divide between people. While there was the richer class that lived in big houses with balconies even, the poorer people lived in thatched mud huts with one room.

When it came to religion, the Guptas like the Mauryans seem to have been quite open. But the hold of Buddhism seemed to be getting weaker during this time. Remember that Hinduism as prescribed in the Vedas had still not reached people in the appropriate manner. What was passed on was majorly the practices of the Aryans who invaded several parts of the country. During the Gupta empire though, the sacrificial and ritualistic practices seem to have driven people away from Aryan imposed religious rites through the ages.

This was the same reason probably that people took on very easily to Buddhism too. But here it would be crucial to mention that even though Buddhism may seem like an easy set of teachings on the surface of it, the teachings do require a deep, constant self-awareness which requires that much dedication too. But in the midst of fulfilling their material needs, they may not have had the time or the mental resources to understand the core doctrines of Buddhism.

And hence local deity practices make a strong comeback. People during the Gupta age had strong Vaishnavite and Shivaite influences. These were still forms of Hinduism but just not as it was practiced in the royal classes. A significant event of this time was that all the Vedic epics that were passed on for generations were now compiled in their final form of literary resources. Thus, the ancient Vedic traditions were now put on record and came under the authority of the Brahmins who were considered to be the learned men.

As this authority grew, the social caste system became more pronounced too. Since the Brahmins were more likely to be the people who read and understood Sanskrit, they came to have a hold over bureaucracy as well as common people. The caste system became much more rigid than it previously was. The caste system that was originally treated as the occupational guideline for smooth functioning now became an imposed, hereditary, unsurpassable restriction passed on over generations.

There were four castes—Brahmins, the learned men, Kshatriyas, the warriors, Vaishyas, the traders, and the merchants, and Shudras, the peasants. There was yet another caste called untouchables who were treated as outcasts and were made to live on the outskirts of the villages so that they would not corrupt the other castes with their impurity. Initially, agriculture was also taken up by the Vaishyas but this changed as time passed by. These castes were initially just occupational groups that ensured all quarters of the society functioned well. People could move between these castes if they felt like it. But this changed during the Gupta age. Though it may not have yet become a social evil in the Gupta period, the seeds for it were certainly sown around this time.

All said and done, though, the Gupta rule is said to have been a time of prosperity and growth like no other. The Guptas had territorial control over rich reserves of iron ore and this could have been the main reason behind their advanced metallurgical techniques. This iron ore was a major component not only in internal use but also in overseas trade. Cities were developed as trading centers and port cities while many others were treated as pilgrimage centers too.

Beautiful temples and monasteries were built across the empire. It must be noted that the famous Nalanda University which would later become a hub for learning was constructed during the Gupta period too. The great poet Kalidasa also lived during these times, though we are not entirely sure of the exact dates. Be it the bold and beautiful erotic sculptures at Khajuraho temples or the paintings at Ajanta caves, they have all been darted back to the patronage of Guptas. Arts, particularly painting, was considered to be a respectable occupation.

Arts and entertainment, however, was not the only accomplishment. This age saw tremendous growth and progress in mathematical, scientific, and medicinal lines thanks to some giants in these fields. Aryabhata was one such name. He was the first mathematician-astronomer-physicist to propose that earth was indeed a sphere rather than a flat surface. His idea of using zero as a figure and even his mention of the relativity of motion have made him immortal even in the modern world of physics and mathematics. Vagbhata was the medical expert who lived during the Gupta times. He is considered to have completed the "great medical trio" who lived in Ancient India—Susruta, a surgeon, and Charaka, a physician. Both these lived much before the Gupta empire but Vagbhata was the one to record his learnings in Ashtanga Samgraha, a compilation of eight different branches of medicine.

The Decline of Guptas

The Gupta empire flourished for around 230 years, leaving significant imprints of its existence on the rest of the events that were to follow. Be it Chandragupta I, Samudragupta, or Chandragupta II, they all provided the Gupta empire with the needed stability with their decades of rule at a time.

Chandragupta I ruled from 320–330 AD, Samudragupta from 335–375 AD, and Chandragupta Vikramaditya from 375–415 AD. That kind of longevity is bound to contribute to at least some part of the Gupta age stability if not all. Chandragupta II, or Chandragupta Vikramaditya as he was fondly called, was then succeeded by Kumaragupta, who again had a peaceful time ruling the empire because of the solid base created over the past many decades.

And then came Skandagupta, during whose reign things started to unravel for Gupta rule. He had to face the unfortunate rebellion of a particular tribe called Pushyamitra. Skandagupta was, no doubt, successful in snubbing the retaliation but it was obvious that the mutiny had left him politically and financially weak. Before the Guptas could heal from this wound, they faced another brutal strike from the Hunas, or the Huns. Again, Skandagupta was successful in driving back these forces. But both these events had left a large gaping hole in the treasuries of the Gupta empire that they were never able to recover from.

The Gupta empire did not die out soon after though. It went on for a few more years when its last ruler Vishnugupta's reign ended. He had ruled from 540–550 AD. There isn't anything known yet about the immediate successors. But one thing we know for certain is that the Gupta rule had lost its "golden" luster long before it ended.

CHAPTER 4
THE CULTURAL SHIFT

Before we move ahead to the beginnings of the medieval period in Indian history, it is essential to consolidate the mammoth changes that were taken from ancient times into medieval times. This is crucial because it is central to understanding the story of India, the perceptions associated with it, as well as the implications these perceptions may have for understanding present-day India.

Until now, we have looked at specific contributions during specific eras. But now, let's take a moment to understand the bigger picture of what Indian culture looked like and how it eventually shifted, rendering some things completely obscure and making others quite conspicuous.

Dharma and Mythology

The Vedic times, despite the time-lapse, continue to have a strong influence on the mindset of the Indian masses even today. A majority of this influence comes from the mythological legends as well as teachings that are passed down from the Vedic period.

Hindu mythology prophesies four eras, or Yugas—Satya Yuga, Treta Yuga, Dwapara Yuga, and lastly Kali Yuga (which is the predicted end of the world). Lord Vishnu holds a special place in this scheme of things. It is believed that Vishnu has ten avatars or incarnations. Every time the world is taken over by evil, Vishnu takes the form of his incarnation and arrives on the earth to defeat evil. Ram and Krishna are believed to be two of those incarnations that appear in Treta and Dwapara Yugas respectively. The two epics are a tribute paid to these incarnations.

As mentioned before, these mythological stories which were initially passed down were documented as literary sources in their final form during the Gupta age. Ramayana and Mahabharata were two of the greatest epics ever written in ancient India. The validity of these epics is certainly shaky at best. Some believe the incidents to be true while others may think of them as completely fictional. Some others might believe that though the events happened, the writers seem to have taken great artistic liberties in their portrayal. Whichever you may choose to believe, it's crucial to be mindful of the line between mythology and history because, without this distinction, we would be treading very dangerous territory.

The Legend of Ram

Ramayana is an epic containing 24,000 verses by Sage Valmiki. This is said to have been originally composed in the fifth century BCE. Ramayana in itself has had a major influence over the religious beliefs of people and hence it is extremely crucial we understand where it came from. While the narrative is a simple story of the victory of good over evil, it presents a number of layers—political, social, ethical—to be analyzed. It is intriguing how Ramayana, as well as Mahabharata, presents great lessons in Dharma or duty. Ram especially has been portrayed as the virtuous hero who put Dharma before everything else. Ramayana is more than anything else a story of Dharma, an ideal state of existence, and Ram is an ideal man.

The story goes something like this: Dasharath, the king of Ayodhya is a great king who has three wives. The eldest queen gives birth to Ram, the middle gives birth to twins,

Lakshman and Shatrughna, and the youngest one births another son named Bharat. In due course, Ram and Lakshman were sent to accompany sage Vishwamitra to help protect his Ashrama from demons. These demons would desecrate the holy rituals with blood and bones and then kill the people performing the sacrifices. Ram and Lakshman, clever, able, and well-trained warriors as they were, defeated the demons and freed the people of the Ashrama of the continued oppression.

After this, the sage took them to the kingdom of Mithila to let them take part in the Swayamvara. This was an event where the prospective grooms had come together to decide who would be the most worthy to be Princess Sita's husband. Ramayana mentions that the king of Mithila, Janak, had found Sita abandoned in a field and had raised her as his own daughter. In this epic, Sita is said to have been born of earth and not much else is mentioned. Janak had decided that Sita would wed the person that successfully lifted Pinaka, the Great Bow of Shiva.

Several men tried but were unsuccessful in moving it even one inch. The ceremony of Swayamvara had gone on for months and the bow remained in its place. The story goes on to mention that even Ravana, the great villain of this legend, had also attempted to pick up the bow. Being a great devotee of Shiva, he was quite certain he would be able to lift it up without any difficulty. Such was his surprise when he found it a terribly difficult task. He picked it up briefly only to drop it and thus was out of the race for Sita's hand. This is said to have bruised his ego beyond words. After all of this, though, when Ram reached the Swayamvara, he is said to have picked it up with ease, and while pulling the string, he broke the bow into two. Everyone was dumbstruck with his strength and he was thus married to Sita with all festivities.

As Dasharath was getting older, he needed a successor and wished for Ram to sit on the throne. Even all his brothers wished for the same thing. Unfortunately, though, the

youngest queen was unhappy as she wished for her own son Bharat to be the king. The hatred in her heart towards Ram was so much that she ordered him to leave Ayodhya and go into exile for 14 years. Dasharath refused but Ram, being the ideal son, had made his decision. Sita and Lakshman followed him into exile for his love.

Ram, Sita, and Lakshman lived the next 14 years in a forest, facing and overcoming many obstacles including dangerous demons along the way. One such demon was Surpanakha, Ravana's sister. Surpanakha is said to have fallen for Ram but being a married man, he told her to talk to Lakshman. Lakshman, making fun of her appearance, refused too. In her fit of anger, she threatened to hurt Sita and in retaliation, Lakshman is said to have shot her nose with an arrow.

In pain, she went to her brother Ravana and all hell broke loose. Ravana saw this as the perfect opportunity to show the world who was more powerful among the two. And thus, he drew a cunning plan to kidnap Sita and thus lure Ram into battle. The story says that Ravana mesmerized Sita with a golden deer outside their hut in the forest. When Ram and Lakshman went to catch the deer at Sita's request, he, Ravana, came in the guise of a hermit. He then took Sita to his kingdom Lanka and imprisoned her there.

Ram, with the help of his great devotee Hanuman, the monkey commander of a monkey army, fought a great battle with Ravana. Ravana is said to have been a great warrior too with many great talents. But his only downfall is said to have been arrogance and ego. After Ram won the battle, he came home with Sita as their exile too had ended. His brother Bharat never ascended the throne, always waiting for his brother to come back.

As things got back to normal, Ram one day heard one of his subjects raise doubts about Sita's purity as he passed by. This kept eating him from within and though he trusted Sita completely, he believed it his duty to dispel all doubts from his subjects' minds. He thus tells Sita to give Agnipariksha, the test of fire, where she would be required to walk through the fire. And since both of them know that she is blameless, she will come out safe and sound. Sita, though terribly hurt, walked through the fire without a scratch on her body. However, after this, rather than returning to the palace, she went into exile once again to live at sage Valmiki's Ashrama. There she gave birth to Ram's two sons, Luv and Kush. After years of exile, Ram found out about his sons and invited them to the palace. But for Sita, he again asked for the same test of sanctity to be proven to his subjects as she had been under the roof of another man all these years. Sita then took the final test and asked the earth to swallow her back to where she came from. The earth shattered open and Sita went away forever.

That is the great Ramayana story. It's not a happy ending but it's certainly one that raises questions as well as answers. Ram's willingness to give up the love of his life solely for the Raj-Dharma, the duty to his kingdom, has been a controversial aspect. But as mentioned before, this is a story of idealism and it delivers exactly what it promises. Also, remember that despite the fantasized elements, the names of the places are quite real. Even many research studies suggest that this might indeed have been inspired by true events.

The Epic of Mahabharata

While Ramayana is a tale of the ideal, Mahabharata is the tale of the real. The characters in this story are flawed much like in real life. This story is about cousins who fought for the right to the throne. This story is much more complex than Ramayana as it weaves in numerous other stories, each with a peculiar philosophical discourse. The epic poem written by Vyasa is 100,000 verses long and composed in the fourth century BCE.

Dhritarashtra, the king of Hastinapura, was married to Gandhari and they both had 100 sons who are called Kauravas, and one daughter. Dhritarashtra's brother Pandu was an excellent warrior who took care of the defense of the state, and after fighting tirelessly, he had retired into the forest with his two wives Kunti and Madri. There he had five sons of his own, collectively known as the Pandavas. When Pandu and Madri died in the forest, Kunti came back to the palace with the five sons, and all 105 princes were trained under their teacher Drona.

During their education, however, enmity started brewing between the two groups. Karn, who was yet another student under Drona and an excellent archer also sided with Duryodhana, the eldest of the Kauravas. As Yudhishtir was the eldest among the 105 princes he inherited the throne. He was also quite popular among the people due to his kind nature—again, always dedicated to Dharma. Duryodhana did not agree to this and he made many attempts on the lives of Kunti and her sons.

The Pandavas went into hiding and survived on the alms given by people. One day they found themselves at the Swayamvar of Draupadi, the beautiful princess of Panchal, seeking alms as usual. The task for the Swayamvar was not easy. There was a pole at the top of which was a fast-spinning fish. The prospective grooms had to shoot the fish by looking at its reflection in the water kept under the pole. No one had been able to make the shot yet, including the Kauravas. Karn was not even given a chance because Draupadi announced that she would not marry someone from an inferior clan. Arjuna, one of the Pandavas, then stepped forward and shot the fish in its eye with five arrows in a single attempt.

Since Arjuna was not the eldest, it was decided that Draupadi would be the common wife to all five Pandavas. As the news of Arjuna's feat traveled, the Pandavas were invited back to Hastinapur and Dhritarashtra decided to divide the kingdom, giving some part to Pandavas and the rest to Kauravas. Though the land given to the Pandavas was barren, they still made it prosper and named it Indraprastha. Jealous of their success, Duryodhana with Uncle Shakuni invited Yudhishtir for a dice game. Shakuni who was to play on Duryodhan's behalf was a skilled player and Yudhishtir lost everything, including his kingdom and wife. Duryodhana even made attempts to disrobe Draupadi in the dice hall full of people. Eventually, Yudhishtir was given the choice to hand over Draupadi or go into a 12-year exile where no one would know who they were. They chose exile.

While on this exile, they came in contact with the king of the Virat kingdom whom they served as servants. It was only when their exile ended did they reveal their Pandava identity. The Virat king then proposed a marriage alliance and Arjuna's son Abhimanyu was married off to the Virat princess. At this point, the battle between Pandavas and Kauravas was unavoidable. Both parties started gathering allies.

The crucial turning point was Krishna coming on to the side of the Pandavas. Krishna was Kunti's brother's son and was thus a cousin to the Pandavas. He was blessed with divine powers and was the greatest strategist. Krishna played the role of Arjuna's charioteer and was largely responsible for the Pandavas' victory despite having much lesser strength in the war.

There are numerous other stories that haven't been touched upon in this context here. But the main difference between the two epics is Ram and Krishna's differences in their approach. While Ram was the ideal one that always followed Dharma, Krishna was the practical one who believed in Karma or the power of action, even if it meant bending the rules here and there. This is particularly important for the philosophical ideology that the epic in particular and Hinduism in general promotes.

Teachings of the Bhagavad Gita

The war at Kurukshetra is said to have raged for 18 whole days. The casualties on both sides were so horrific that this was named Mahabharata, the Great Indian War. The Pandavas won, thanks to Krishna being on their side. But unfortunately, almost all their family is said to have died, including the Kauravas. After this, the Pandavas reigned for almost 36 years with Dharma (duty towards their subjects).

One of the most important outcomes of this war was the recitation of the Bhagavad Gita by Lord Krishna to Arjuna. Literally translated to "the song of the Lord," it is said to have dissipated the guilt and angst in Arjuna's mind about fighting his own brothers. It is one of the most crucial texts of Hinduism and is in widespread use even today. The life lessons from the Gita have been used even in management teams as philosophical rather than religious principles. Moreover, in its translations from Sanskrit to several Indian as well as foreign languages, it has also served as the easiest form of introduction to Hinduism as a philosophical religion to anyone who would be interested.

Though it is now a part of the Mahabharata epic, many historians believe that it wasn't added to the main epic until later. Thus, while the Gita is believed to have been composed in the fourth century BC, the Bhagavad Gita is likely to have been added in the second century BC. Gita, in simple words, is a conversation between the troubled warrior Arjuna and the all-knowing Lord Krishna. Arjuna poses questions and moral dilemmas which Krishna then resolves with his wisdom as well as the basic principles mentioned in the Vedas.

In essence, when Arjuna refuses to take up arms against his brothers and continues to despair about having to kill his brothers, Krishna talks to him about the soul or Atma that lies beyond the cycle of birth and death. Getting attached to anything and anyone in between this and birth and death only increases the suffering of the souls. It is for this reason that one should keep performing his duty (Dharma) without getting attached to the outcome. These expectations and attachment often hold the individual prisoner when they start thinking of "doing" something rather than something that just needs to be done. Krishna thus enlightens Arjuna that the battle must be fought because it is the right thing. It is because of this knowledge that Arjuna goes on to pick up his bow and arrow and the Pandavas eventually win the war.

Philosophical Roots

It must be noted that the philosophical beginnings of Hinduism are not to be attributed to the Gita. Rather the Gita is the compilation of the philosophy mentioned in the Vedas, a summary if you will. Hinduism, before it got muddled with ritualistic practices under the Brahmanical influence, was indeed a set of philosophies, a way of life, rather than an organized religion. It encourages its followers to gain "true knowledge" that will help set them free.

The Hindu philosophy looks at the universe in terms of two entities—Brahman and Atman. Brahman is the ultimate reality, the highest principle in the Universe. It is what we are made of and what we eventually turn into. It is the one thing that binds us all together. Atman, on the other hand, is the fraction of the Brahman that is within our soul. As long as we are caught in the cycle of birth and death, Atman is prevented from reuniting with Brahman. Once the soul attains salvation or Moksha though, it goes back to the Brahman.

The attachments that we develop through our lifetime mask this ultimate reality and keep us engaged in meaningless matters. Thus, the purpose of life must be to get rid of these illusions of control and gain true knowledge. For this, it is necessary to look inward and discover the power that comes with that knowledge. The only way to attain salvation is through Yoga (the union of body and soul). Four paths of this union have been identified in the Hindu philosophy—Bhakti Yoga (path of devotion), Jnana Yoga (path of knowledge), Karma Yoga (path of action and duty), and Raja Yoga (the royal path of meditation).

It's no secret that these are abstract concepts that may not be easy to grasp for everyone. Top that with being written in Sanskrit and it's obvious why the Brahmins captured most authority.

Culture and Life in Ancient India

Life in ancient India seems to have been strongly driven by their philosophical orientation. They followed what is known as the Ashrama system. Ashramas are places that were built by sages and acted as resting places for travelers along the way. Using the same analogy, in the Ashrama Dharma, these stages are like the resting places you need to live at and nourish your soul, in order to travel ahead. In this system, every individual's life is divided into four stages or four Ashramas—Brahmacharya (the learning/student phase), Grihastha (the householder phase), Vanaprastha (the retirement phase), and lastly Sanyasa (the phase of renunciation). Every individual regardless of their gender, caste, or occupation goes through these phases.

The Hindu philosophy believes that every individual must fulfill four goals in their lifetime—Dharma (duty), Artha (material wealth), Kama (pleasure), and Moksha (salvation). Some may find it contradictory that Hinduism, on one hand, advocates detachment, and on the other, assumes pleasure and wealth as goals of life. But it is intriguing that this philosophy doesn't expect its followers to stick to abstract ideals but shows them a way in which they can move through the worldly phases of life while ultimately aiming for salvation.

This Ashrama Dharma led to the concept of Gurukuls, which were Ashramas where children would be sent during their Brahmachraya phase. It is estimated that in ancient times even girls and children from lower castes were educated in these Gurukuls. But as the Brahmanical, patriarchal influences increased, these educational institutes became reserved only for boys belonging to upper classes.

Once the education was completed, the individual was expected to get married and take up the responsibilities of his family—earn enough money, raise children, and protect his wife.

As his children grew up—sons educated and daughters married off—he then moved into Vanaprastha Ashrama. Here, most men left their homes and retired into forests. They lived off the alms given to them by the people in nearby villages. This was supposed to be the beginning of detachment after having had the opportunity to experience the worldly pleasures of intimacy and attachment.

Last came the Sanyasa phase where the individual would retreat further into the forest and would gradually give up food and sleep in favor of Dhyana or meditation. These people would then take a Samadhi. This would be a state of existence where, while in their physical body, they would still be able to connect to the ultimate reality eliminating the need for physical sustenance eventually.

When we analyze the big ancient Indian picture it is clear that apart from certain evils that were breeding in the murky name of rituals and social order, there was also widespread openness in terms of religious and social beliefs. The Indian philosophy, for the most part, seems to have been "live and let live." However, this was majorly jeopardized when iconoclastic policies followed by the Mughal invasions resulted in a paradigm shift about how religion was viewed.

PART II
MEDIEVAL INDIA

In this part, we explore the period from the 6th century to the 19th century, as one by one great emperor and shrewd explorers invaded the Indian subcontinent to establish legendary empires and to gain supremacy over the exotic Indian treasures.

IV

CHAPTER 5
THE MUGHAL SULTANATE

After the fall of Guptas, the Hun invasions were common but Indian kings like Baladitya, a later Gupta, and Harsha of the Vardhanas successfully defeated them. The latter went on to establish a handsome empire stretched across North India from 606–647 AD. A Chinese traveler by the name of Hiuen Tsang wrote an elaborate account of his visit to Harsha Vardhana's kingdom and its social, economic, and political prosperity. However, Harsha Vardhana had no heirs and after his death, the empire quickly disintegrated into several smaller kingdoms. Interestingly, now the epicenter of the territorial campaigns was shifting to South India and multiple dynasties fought for dominance, Chalukyas and Kadambas leaving an imprint.

Another significant development that was to

change the course of not just Indian but global history was the emergence of Islam. The prophet Muhammad was born in 570 AD in Mecca, and when he was around 40 years old, the divine truth was revealed to him. His disciples then traveled around the world with the Arab forces, spreading the message of Islam. The Arab forces soon annihilated the mighty Byzantine empire despite having not much battle experience. The Arab forces progressed with surprising speed and agility, making dents all along the way.

The Arabs invaded Sind in the seventh century and were often called Yavanas, Tajiks, and Turuskas. However, as mentioned earlier, the Indian tradition was so open that the notorious intentions of the Arabs to conquer with monotheistic religious ideas went largely unnoticed. These were merely treated and repelled as isolated invasions rather than a socio-political campaign against the followers of other religious beliefs. Of course, along with ignorance, there was the complacency that eventually led to the downfall of many Indian rulers. Having said that though, the time period between these invasions was characterized by quite peaceful relations between the Arabs and the locals. Whether these were a part of a larger political plan or not, these invasions essentially led the Indian subcontinent into the medieval Mughal era of its maturity.

Babur

Babur was the first Mughal emperor and a descendant of the infamous Genghis Khan as well as Timur. He assumed a position of power quite early in his life at the age of merely 11 years. He ascended the throne of Fergana (present-day Uzbekistan) when his father passed away. His uncles tried relentlessly to dethrone him but this little boy still went on to establish an empire that would rule for centuries in India.

With constant setbacks in battle and mutinies back home, Babur eventually turned his attention away from his state of origin and started moving east in the hopes of finding a kingdom to rule. He believed that due to his descendence from Timur, he was the rightful heir to the Sayyid dynasty led by Khizr Khan. Khizr Khan was initially left in charge by Timur of his feudal acquisition in Punjab. Even with the twisted logic, there was yet another flaw in Babur's plans. The Sayyid dynasty had already been ousted by Ibrahim Lodhi. But Babur was a man on a mission and eventually defeated Ibrahim Lodhi in 1526.

He, thus, became the Sultan of the Sultanate consisting of Delhi and Agra. Lodhi, however, was not the last of Babur's worries. The Indian Rajputs, especially Rana Sanga of Mewar, were putting on a strong front. But when Sanga died, possibly poisoned by one of his own men, Babur's road to consolidation was cleared. He immediately began his expansion strategy with the latest weapons like guns and cannons. This gave him a huge advantage over his enemies.

He was a lover of the arts and showed a deep appreciation of the various Indian structures. He writes about these in his autobiography Baburnama which in itself was a milestone none of the other Mughal emperors had yet achieved. However, this liberalism did not seem to translate to religious figures. He displays blatant anger towards "naked" Jain idols that he ordered be destroyed. Even the Guru Granth Sahib, the holy scripture of Sikhs, written by Guru Nanak, lists a number of brutalities unleashed by Babur on his subjects. But the same scripture goes on to mention that Babur called to meet Guru Nanak after hearing his song. In that conversation, when Guru Nanak stood up to him and advised him to free the prisoners and be a just king, Babur is said to have repented for his sins. The legend even claims that he let the prisoners go and changed his ways. However, mixed his legacy, his name has surely been etched in history.

Humayun

When Babur died after a prolonged illness in 1530, his son Humayun inherited the Mughal empire. The empire stretched over present-day Afghanistan, Pakistan, Northern India, and Bangladesh. Despite the vastness of this empire, Humayun was still battling the ghosts of his father's rule. The Mughals had not yet been accepted by their subjects as their rulers. The battles of Panipat, Khanua, and Ghaghara were some of the fiercest battles fought.

Humayun continued to be challenged too. He was first called into battle in 1535 by Bahadur Shah of Gujarat. Humayun occupied Gujarat but had to fight off Bahadur Shah every now and then. This threat was neutralized only in 1537, but Humayun's worries were far from over and Sher Shah of Sur defeated Humayan twice, first in Chausa in 1539 and later in Kannauj in 1540. This marked the end of Humayun's first stint in India. However, there was more to come. After going back to

Iran, he again consolidated a bigger army with the help of Shah Tahmasp and besieged Kandahar in 1545. He then began his march back to India, winning Lahore in 1555 and in a few months securing his place at the throne of Delhi and Agra.

He is said to have been a patron of several long-lasting observatories. He also was responsible for promoting the development of the Safavid style of painting characteristic of the Mughal culture in India. Like his father, his life was also chronicled in a biographical form by his sister Gulbadan Begum. Even his death seems to signify his love for books. He is said to have died by a fatal fall from the staircase of his library when he was coming down, his arms full of books.

Akbar (1556–1605)

Akbar, Humayun's son, inherited the Mughal throne at the almost ripe age of 14. He was thus mentored and advised until he came of age by Bairam Khan, an advisor of the Mughals. Akbar is hailed by most as an able and ambitious leader. He undertook multiple campaigns and made special efforts to transform the meager kingdom left to him by his father. He didn't merely conquer territories but ensured that his subjects were also loyal to him. He revised the tax structure so as to put no added financial pressures on non-Muslims. He even reduced the "tribute taxes" levied on the Rajput kings. The result of this was that Akbar was spending less time putting out fires all over the place and more time strategizing, administering, and executing.

Akbar also expanded the empire through marriage alliances regardless of religion. Though it was a common practice to marry the Hindu princesses to Muslim conquerors, this was often done as a means of humiliating the Hindu royal class into submission. However, when Akbar married Jodha Bai, a Rajput princess, the men in her family were made members of his royal court, the same as his Muslim in-laws. This earned him loyalty and respect amongst his allies. Of course, it is not unimaginable that some people were against this kind of integration.

Akbar was a truly multicultural emperor. He is said to have built within Fatehpur Sikri (the walled city with Persian architecture that he had designed) a temple or Ibadat Khana where he frequently met with learned men from other religions. He even allowed the construction of a church in Agra during his time. He is also associated with a faith he himself established called Din-i-Ilahi which combined elements from Islam, Hinduism, and Zoroastrianism. However, this never caught on. Regardless, he himself expressed openness and tolerance towards all religions, even participating in festivals of other faiths.

Akbar was not an artist himself but this never stopped him from appreciating art and talent whenever he saw it. He is well-known for his patronage of the Navratnas, or the nine gems in his court—Abul Fazl, the biographer and author of Akbarnama, Abul Faizi, a scholar, Tansen, a singer, Raja Birbal, the witty advisor, Raja Man Singh, the lieutenant, Abdul Rahim Khan-I-Khana, a poet, and Fagir Aziao-Din and Mulla Do Piaza, two more advisors.

Some historians believe that Jahangir may have poisoned his own father so as to gain control of the powerful throne.

Jahangir (1605–1627)

It is said that when Akbar died, Jahangir's son Khusrau Mirza was considered for the position. However, Jahangir took over instead and began ruling within a few days of Akbar's death. On most accounts, he seemed to have an ambitious attitude, similar to his father. Though Akbar had expanded the Mughal empire, there were pockets within that empire that had not yet pledged allegiance to the Mughals, such as the Mewar province. One of Jahangir's greatest victories was the resolution of this conflict.

It is said that Jahangir had many wives, some say close to 20. These were marriages for the purposes of alliances with the Rajputs. In 1611, he is said to have married Mehr-un-Nisa who he later named Nur Jahan. Nur Jahan was a beautiful, smart, strong woman well-trained in the art of war. She was known to have a strong influence over Jahangir's court matters as well as to have led the army into the battlefield.

As for Jahangir's views on religion, he seems to have had an ambiguous stance. While he didn't exact any additional taxes from non-Muslims or even give any special powers to Muslims in his court, he also showcased instances of specific hate crimes towards some Hindus and Sikhs. For example, he executed the Fifth Sikh Guru, Guru Arjan Dev, resulting in friction between Muslims and Sikhs. He is also said to have tortured Hindu men for marrying Muslim girls in Kashmir. This suggests that he agreed with interfaith marriages only as long as they resulted in conversion to Islam.

After Jahangir passed away, Nur Jahan took up the mantle of the emperor. Well, almost. When she started issuing royal mandates in her name, Jahangir's son Khurram, who would later be called Shah Jahan, imprisoned her for the rest of her days.

Shah-Jahan (1628–1658)

Legend has it that even though Akbar's first wife didn't have any children of her own, she was told by a psychic that she would still raise a future Sultan, and Akbar had the intuition that Khurram, Jahangir's third son, would be that future Sultan. This resulted in a strong bond between Akbar and Khurram. In 1607, he was engaged to Arjumand Banu Begum. However, their marriage was halted due to, again, a prediction made by the fortune teller. In the meantime, he was married off to two other princesses for the purpose of political alliances. He had one son each with those wives. But it is said that his heart remained with Arjumand Banu. When they got married, they went on to birth 14 children, seven of whom made it to adulthood.

Shah Jahan had already proved his mettle as a leader and warrior. He followed an expansion policy in a steadfast manner. While he aligned himself with some Rajput kings such as those of Mewar and Bundelkhand, he took it upon himself to destroy the others like the Rajputs from Bundela. He also involved his son Aurangzeb in his military operations in South India, and the boundaries of the empire widened to include Golconda and Bijapur.

Despite all the military success, one would have to admit that Shah Jahan's most important contribution to history is his larger-than-life tribute to his wife Mumtaz—the Taj Mahal. Even today, people flock to Agra to bear witness to the beauty of this white marble monument. But that wasn't the only thing he had built. Red Fort and Jama Masjid in New Delhi and Shalimar Gardens in Lahore are only a couple of the many structures he commissioned.

When Mumtaz died after birthing her 14th child, Shah Jahan was shattered. It is said that he isolated himself for almost a year. When he did emerge at the behest of one of his daughters, his hair had gone gray beyond measure at the early age of 40.

He went on to rule until 1658 when he fell ill. One of his sons, Dara Shikoh, took up his duties while he recovered. His other son Aurangzeb had different plans. He was furious that he wasn't called upon for assuming the emperor's role. Having been Shah Jahan's governor, he was already skilled at warfare and had an army at hand. He marched on to defeat Dara Shikoh and won. He then went on to imprison Shah Jahan until he breathed his last in 1666.

Aurangzeb (1658–1707)

Aurangzeb is likely the most hated Mughal king in Indian history. He imposed increasingly puritanical practices which were the hallmark of a religious fanatic. Some historians prefer to look at Aurangzeb's reign as divided into two parts. In the first part, between 1658 to about 1680, Aurangzeb was viewed as a skilled and vicious ruler, never loved but respected and feared all the same. During this time, he was observed to be busy protecting his borders from Persians and Turks. A hint of complacency is visible in the manner in which he dealt with Shivaji, the chief of the Maratha kingdom.

Aurangzeb didn't know it yet but this chief was to be a large part of the decline of the Mughal empire.

Somewhere around 1680, one can see a clear shift in Aurangzeb's attitude when he started practicing bigotry with his subjects. The poll taxes on non-Muslims which were abolished by Akbar were brought back and tolerance had been wiped clean from the Mughal empire. He even imposed the Islamic Sharia law on the entire empire. This became the major cause for dissatisfaction and even hatred amongst his non-Muslim subjects who were still in a majority throughout the empire. The mutinies and the uprisings that began with the Marathas soon caught up with the Rajputs as well as the Sikhs, but the Marathas still remained Aurangzeb's biggest worry. Even after the dissipation of the Maratha kingdom, the Maratha soldiers that were left behind employed guerilla warfare to disturb Aurangzeb's peace. This worked wonders as even towards the end of his rule he was obsessed with catching up to the Marathas.

Maratha Wars and the Decline of the Mughal Empire

While Aurangzeb was the wealthiest and the most powerful Mughal ruler of all, he also was the reason that the empire was eventually razed to the ground. As mentioned above, Marathas were his most formidable opponents yet, especially under the able and inspiring leadership of Shivaji. Aurangzeb hoped to employ Akbar's old technique with the Marathas—conquer and reconcile. However, this would not succeed with Shivaji. Shivaji had already humbled the likes of Shaista Khan by cutting off his fingers at the Lal Mahal in Pune.

In 1666, Shivaji was invited, rather summoned to Agra to be forced into negotiation and eventually submission. He was to be kept under house arrest until he gave in. But Shivaji made a supremely clever escape and left Aurangzeb fuming. This game of cat and mouse continued with not only Shivaji but all of the Maratha descendants. Aurangzeb had poured so much of the Mughal treasury into these small battles that it had left the Mughal empire quite hollow from within.

Aurangzeb is considered to be the last of the effective monarchs who held the vast empire under them. He had, after all, ruled for 49 years.

But unfortunately, his extremist policies had already done permanent damage and it would be impossible for his son and successor Bahadur Shah I to repair any of what was shattered. The massive Mughal empire collapsed in the 18th century and its legacy went down with it.

CHAPTER 6
THE EAST INDIAN COMPANY

Towards the end of the 16th century, the British crown was in desperate need of money and it had found the perfect solution to resolve all their financial concerns. They were to set up trading posts in the East Indies as they called it and gain access to valuable exotic items like spices, metals, tobacco, and so on. Not only that, they would then grant access to only certain traders to trade in that area, exacting some fees and commissions from them too. Overseas travel was a risky business after all. So, the traders preferred to reduce the competition as much as possible.

This idea came to life on December 31st, 1600 when Queen Elizabeth I, with an official charter, granted one group of merchants exclusive trading rights in India. This group of merchants called themselves the East India Company. However, it didn't take much to understand that this was to be the front behind which British imperialism would creep into the Indian subcontinent.

However, Britain was not the first to see an opportunity. Spanish and Portuguese traders had already established their own trading posts, and the British Crown was somewhat paranoid that this could be the determining factor for their power politics. Even they themselves couldn't have imagined how valuable the East Indian Company (EIC) would be in their colonial strategy.

The EIC was founded by two merchants, John Watts and George White. It made its first voyage to India under the command of Sir James Lancaster. The company at this time was still exploring its options for establishing a base for its operations. After the Battle of Swally in 1612 with the Portuguese in Surat, India seemed to be a more and more feasible and profitable prospect. By this time, they had already built their first factory in Masulipatnam in Andhra Pradesh, with the next to come up in 1613 in Surat.

During the time of this development, a large part of the Indian subcontinent was being ruled by Jahangir. The EIC officials were at first viewed as mere supplicants who wanted to establish favorable trading relations. The trading relations would be important, at least in the beginning, especially because the South-East Asian market had already proved difficult for the EIC, due to the strong influence of the Dutch East India Company. Now the EIC traders knew that they would require all the support they could from the local powers. For the first few initial journeys, the Company raised its joint stock separately. This only meant that the risks of the voyage, as well as the ownership of the Company, were shared between different stakeholders. However, after 1657 a permanent joint stock was raised, indicating it was in India for the long haul.

An Era of Exploitation

Corruption and ruthless profiteering seem to have been breeding in the Company from the very beginning. Though the Crown gave an exclusive trading monopoly to the EIC, the Company would still go on to allow its voyagers private trading. This was done under the pretense of giving them added incentives so they would make the dangerous voyage to India. This marked the beginning of conniving exchanges under the flag of the EIC.

It has been noted by many historians that the Company was becoming an increasingly well-oiled exploitative machine with its official company trades and unofficial private trades making a fortune at the cost of the Indian locals. However, this was only the first step. With the passing years, the company's involvement with the Indian subcontinent increased.

The first Company ambassador, Thomas Roe, approached Jahangir in 1612 for permission to reside and build factories in Surat. Jahangir's fascination with European rarities seems to have made the task much easier. The traders now knew that they had a safe path to more authority only if they provided the rulers with something of value in return. With the simple ruse of ingratiating the rulers, the Company officials secured several favors like the abolition of the custom duties. This meant that the Company could engage in unlimited trade of exotic materials without the fear of retribution. The worst part was unlike the previous rulers who spent what they earned in the subcontinent itself, a new order was in the making where the wealth from India was headed straight to the Crown.

Most of the 17th century passed in trading ruthlessly in Indian goods, battling the influence of Dutch East India Company, and also eventually warring with elements of the Mughal empire, particularly Shaista Khan, only to lose and pay fines to Aurangzeb. But while all of this was happening, there were also important developments happening back in Britain. The traders who had amassed infinite fortunes had now gone back to England and created a political climate that gave massive advantage to British trade. By the 18th century, specifically after the Battle of Plassey in 1757, the East India Company established itself as a formidable army rather than a trading company. The battle was fought in the village of Palashi, in Maharashtra. The defeat of Bengal Nawab Siraj-ud-Daula marked the beginning of formal British rule in India.

The Fall of the Honorable Company

The Battle of Plassey gave the British administrators infinite powers over the local functioning. They could now make their own rules for trade and even exact taxes as they saw fit. These were the two biggest forms of revenue for the British Crown. From there the British rule only grew from strength to strength. However, the same could not be said for the Company's future. Back in the British Parliament, there seemed to be a heated debate over the running of the EIC in India and the foul practices it engaged in. Rampant corruption among officials kept surfacing. The first Governor-General of Bengal, Warren Hastings, was even tried for misconduct and demands were made that he should be impeached. Ultimately, he was acquitted but the cracks were openly visible.

The final straw came a few decades later when the "Honorable" Company, as it was so often called, engaged in quite a dishonorable act of leveraging illegal drugs. China was quite famous for its tea which is exported for silver. But the Crown's silver reserves were virtually non-existent. Thus, the Company traders used the illicit production of opium in India and traded it in exchange for Chinese tea. Opium, being a banned substance in China, triggered "the Opium Wars" between China and the British traders. The first war was fought between 1839 and 1842 while the second one was between 1856–1860.

Better weaponry gave the British an easy win but exposed the cruel intentions of these traders. The fact that the Chinese were coerced into legalizing the opium trade and that the Indian laborers were enslaved for opium production did not sit well with the British Parliament. To add to the list of cruelties, it came to the fore that the EIC had slaughtered those who protested against such brutal slavery in the Indian Mutiny of 1857. The British Parliament refused to renew their contracts and thus the EIC was disbanded in 1858.

The Uprising of 1857

The Indian Mutiny, sometimes also known as the Sepoy Mutiny, broke out in 1857. This was the first-ever widespread resistance to British advances. Though it bore no success, it sent the message to the British Government that the Indian subjects were certainly not as mute and meek as they had expected. The EIC with its unethical practices and oppressive policies had had it coming a long time. A score of different factors impacted this—the social conditions, the oppressive taxation structure, discrimination of Indian soldiers, and so on.

The spark that lit the Company on fire was the use of greased cartridges. There was a rumor that the grease used in cartridges was made from the fats of cows and pigs. To load these, the soldiers had to bite off the ends of the cartridges.

This violated both the Hindus and Muslims in whose respective religions consumption of cows and pigs was a sin. Sepoy Mangal Pandey was the first to refuse to use these cartridges and attacked the senior officials. He was hanged on the 8th of April that year.

The fire had been lit. After Pandey, there were several more soldiers from Meerut who refused to use the cartridge too. They were also subjected to long and harsh prison sentences. The Indian soldiers had now had enough. They rebelled by shooting several British officials on May 10th and then marched to Delhi to nominate the frail Mughal king Bahadur Shah II as their ruler. This pattern of revolution followed throughout the northern stretch of the country resulting in fatal consequences for the British officials as well as their families. Only a handful of rulers like Nana Sahib, Rani Lakshmibai, and General Bakht Khan took part in the mutiny while other princes held their silence. The violence reached a point where the British officials took brutal action against the soldiers on mere suspicion even when no violent advances were made. The British engaged in planned and despicable vengeance, far more than the acts of the soldiers had warranted. Eventually, peace was declared in July 1859.

The British Parliament realized that it would be impossible to keep matters running smoothly as before with the same administrators. An extensive house cleaning exercise was undertaken and thus the decision to disband the East India Company.

The British Raj

The Indian Mutiny was significant for several reasons. One, it led to major structural changes in the British administration. Two, it led the British rulers to engage in a method of policy-making that would require more participation from their Indian subjects. And three, it led to the complete collapse of the traditional monarch-subject relationship that had existed for several centuries in India. While most of the princes stood as the silent spectators to the mutiny, a new realization had dawned on the laypeople that the kings would not be their saviors, rather it was upon their shoulders to save their nations from the plundering foreigners. This realization was also due to the emerging "middle class" from the influence of the Western class system.

It is clear that the first two results mentioned above were more of face-saving strategies to pacify the Indians. But what the British didn't realize was that when combined with the third factor, it would prove to be a fatal blend for their imperialism. The seeds of nationalism had been sown and over the next 90 years or so these seeds grew into a massive tree. The British Raj continued in India from 1858 to 1947, until independence. Volumes of information can be written about this period alone.

The British administration now followed a policy of non-interference in religious as well as royal matters. The princes were appeased by giving them the "freedom" to choose their successors—as long as they pledged allegiance to the British Crown. The Christian missionaries were required to stop proselytizing. This was not due to a change of heart but a fear that protests may break out again.

The British rule in India continued to harness all its power and wealth from three sources—the taxes levied on agricultural yield, the opium trade with China, and the taxes on salt. As the British population of officials and their families in the country increased, hospitals and educational institutes began appearing too. A great contribution of the British to Indian history was the laying of nationwide railroads. Efforts were made, at least on the surface, to integrate the Indian population within the British ranks. Discrimination was nowhere close to ending but the British were putting up a solid front.

PART III
MODERN INDIA

Here we look at the developments of the 20th century and India's march into a new phase of peace and protests. We understand the tough path towards freedom in all its intricacy.

CHAPTER 7
THE FIGHT FOR FREEDOM

The Nationalist Movement in India took root in 1885 when the Indian National Congress (INC) held its first convention. Founded by a civil servant named A.O. Hume, it was attended by several Indians who were educated in the British tradition like Dadabhai Naoroji, Romesh Chunder Dutt, Surendranth Bannerjee, and so on. The initial Congressman demanded representation in the British administration. Dadabhai Naoroji even went on to be elected as a member of the British House of Commons. They sought the path of dialog and deliberation with the British regarding the policies so as to come to those that would be best for their fellow Indians. The INC was to become the party that possessed a strong influence throughout the freedom struggle.

Although, there were others who did not quite agree. Bal Gangadhar Tilak was the first to sound out the call of Swaraj, or self-rule. He was of the opinion that colonial education was doing a disservice to Indian culture and should therefore be renounced completely. He and other followers of this school of thought believed that there could be no compromise. They declared that Indians were capable of governing themselves and that the British would have to leave for India to be truly independent.

These two schools of thought continued to

have clashes all through the freedom struggle. It was observed that more and more people were becoming radicalized due to the continued oppression of their fellow countrymen by British officials. The Swadeshi Movement (1903–1908) in response to the administrative decision to partition Bengal proved that Indians were now standing up to the imperial powers. Tilak was arrested for his radical views and sentenced to six years imprisonment in Mandalay, Burma. After his release in 1914, he, along with Annie Besant, would lead the Home Rule Movement which lasted between 1916–1918. The freedom struggle had begun and the people would settle for nothing less.

Gandhi and His Mass Appeal

Mohandas Karamchand Gandhi, fondly known as Mahatma Gandhi, has been one of the

biggest influences on the struggle for

independence. Until he arrived on the scene, there were only two ways to respond to the British: fight or compromise. He brought in the third and, in its own way, most revolutionary response—Satyagraha, or non-violent resistance. There are, of course, multiple perceptions regarding his style of leadership, and he may even be considered a pacifist by right-wing thinkers. But whatever the disagreements may be regarding his style, no one can deny the fact that here was a man who had brought people together like no one else ever before. Followers were drawn to him regardless of their religion, caste, and creed, and all the freedom struggle needed at the time was a leader like this at the helm steering the diverse ship.

After having been a victim of racism and discrimination in South Africa, Gandhi decided to dedicate himself to the freedom struggle. Many have called Gandhi's legacy out for being a racist himself but the fact that he did lead India head-first into a new phase of the fight for independence cannot be erased. His first foray into this movement was when the British Government passed the Rowlatt Act of 1919 permitting the officials to detain indefinitely and sentence the accused without a trial. This enraged Gandhi and he thus called an Anti-

Rowlatt Satyagraha. This would mean that people would engage in peaceful meetings. The Government came down hard on these resulting in violence all over.

Jallianwala Bagh Massacre

Millions rose up to Gandhi's call and organized peaceful protests. In Punjab, two leaders were arrested for such protests, Dr. Saifuddin Ketchlew and Dr. Satya Pal. Discontent was evident among people. A week later, thousands of people gathered again in Jallianwala Bagh, peacefully protesting the arrests of their leaders. The British authorities decided to thwart these protests again. One General Dyer reached the grounds where the meeting was in progress. He ordered the only exit be shut off, and then opened fire. It was raining bullets as men, women, and children screamed in agony. But such was the anger against the government that rather than die from Dyer's bullet, they chose to kill themselves by jumping off in a well that was on the ground. More than 2,000 were massacred that day, and this was one of the turning points that was to shape the ideas of many of the revolutionaries in the future. This was also the time when Gandhi concluded that complete independence was the only way things would change.

The Non-Cooperation Movement

This was the first mass movement headed by Gandhi. After Jallianwala Bagh, Gandhi realized that it would not be enough to only tell the government that there was disagreement but there would need to be sufficient impact. Thus, he called on all Indians to stop going to work and to stop using products that were not made in India. Gandhi, with a Charkha (a device to spin yarn), is a common image in the historic symbology of modern India. He made his own Khaki clothes and urged people to do the same.

Beginning in 1920, this movement incorporated men, women, and kids and gained massively from this all-around contribution and participation. They now had the option to fight for freedom with something routine that they could do rather than something huge and heroic. The only instruction they had to follow was Ahimsa, or non-violence.

The movement went on for two years and was becoming a bigger worry by the day for the British. Unfortunately, however, the non-violent movement turned violent as a group of extremists burned down a police station in 1922 in Chauri Chaura, Uttar Pradesh. Several policemen were killed and Gandhi called off the movement completely. Gandhi was then arrested on the charge of sedition and imprisoned for six years.

After this, many people broke off from Gandhi, unhappy with his unilateral decision to call off the movement because of one incident. Many even thought that he did it so he wouldn't have to take the blame for the Chauri Chaura violence.

The Revolutionary Called Bhagat Singh

Bhagat Singh was born on September 28th, 1907, and grew up in an environment of political awareness and debate. He was an articulate man and frequently wrote for publications in his college. He was an atheist who found himself drawn to Marx's ideas of communism. It was no surprise that he did not align with the Gandhian philosophy of non-violence. Not that he advocated violence, but he did believe that sometimes resorting to violence may be the only option there was. It was because of his radical ideas that he got on the British officials' radar. He was arrested once on the suspicion of his involvement in a bomb explosion but then released on bail.

When the Simon Commission was set up in 1928, Indians reacted with tremendous anger. This commission was set up to review the Government of India Act of 1919. This act was originally passed with the intent of getting more Indians to participate in the Government. This was to be in effect for ten years. Ironically, though, the commission set to review it had no Indian representation at all which eventually led to the boycott of the Simon Commission. On its arrival, it was met with black flags and the protest was led by a senior leader of the independence movement known as Lala Lajpat Rai. Though the crowd was completely peaceful, the British reacted with brutal force opening a lathi charge. Rai was severely injured along with many others. Eventually, Rai succumbed to his injuries, further aggravating the others.

Bhagat Singh and Chandrashekar Azad, another revolutionary, decided to avenge Rai's death. They planned to assassinate James Scott who had ordered the lathi charge. They carried out the assassination as planned but in the case of mistaken identity had killed John Saunders.

The killing was condemned by all but Bhagat Singh managed to escape.

However, in 1929, Bhagat Singh, along with his friend Sukhdev decided to detonate a bomb in the Chamber of Deputies, Paris, and turn themselves in because they wanted a trial. They wished for the people to hear all they had to say. The bomb was harmless but injured a few people. Bhagat Singh and Sukhdev had plenty of opportunities to escape but chose not to, and remained in place shouting "Inquilab Zindabad," or "Long Live Revolution!" He was charged with terrorism and eventually hanged on March 23rd, 1931.

Bhagat Singh knew very well what was in store for him and yet he chose to go that path because he wanted to express his ideology. He was of the opinion that you can kill a person but not ideologies.

Civil Disobedience Movement

Gandhi began this movement in 1930 a little after he was released from jail. After the earlier non-cooperation movement, this time it was intended to be a notch higher. This time the movement was to break certain laws in a peaceful manner. Gandhi would march from Sabarmati Ashram in Gujarat to Dandi to oppose the ridiculous taxation structure of the

British. He and his followers marched almost 390 kilometers for 25 days. The people of India were burdened with very high salt taxes and this was impacting people at the very grass-roots level. Thus, Gandhi marched all the way to Dandi shore, and on April 6th, 1930 he held out the salt on the shores in his hand. Thus began the civil disobedience movement. But salt was only a part of it. Girls and women picketed liquor shops and opium trading dens. In some states, entire villages refused to pay "protection taxes" to the local guards. In short, taxation was boycotted on a large scale.

Gandhi was imprisoned again on May 5th, 1930 and the nation turned upset and violent. The Government in turn kept getting more and more repressive which did not help the situation. The Purna Swaraj (complete independence) slogan was now ripe with excitement.

Gandhi-Irwin Pact

Gandhi was released in January 1931. The then Viceroy of India, Lord Irwin, had a fair grasp of the influence Gandhi exercised over people. As the movement gained more steam, he offered to negotiate with Gandhi the terms of the truce, of sorts. Hopeful and optimistic as he was, Gandhi agreed and called for ending the movement. This angered many people because the movement that was turning successful was being called off only on the back of a possibility. People felt disillusioned and disappointed.

The Gandhi-Irwin Pact was signed in 1931 which said that in return for ending the civil disobedience, India would be allowed to participate in the Second Round Table Conference, all political leaders would be released (except for terrorists like Bhagat Singh who was in prison at the time waiting for his death sentence), and the coastal people would be allowed to make salt for personal consumption.

Gandhi was saddened by Bhagat Singh's sentence even though he did not agree with his methods. He did whatever he could to try to save him from being executed. He wrote a fervent letter to Irwin who was also his friend. Even Irwin requested the British judge to reassess the situation. But the British Raj was in turmoil as people were finding their voice and raising it fearlessly. The British administration considered it an opportune time to make an example out of the three young revolutionaries.

Freedom, At Last

The Indian sentiment kept getting more and more intense. Unfortunately for the British, as

World War II raged at a global level, Civil Disobedience was taken to a whole new level where Gandhi encouraged people to refuse to be part of the war under the British flag. Since the war was fought for the basic democratic rights of citizens, Gandhi reasoned that Indians had no place in the war. The Quit India Movement was initiated in August 1942. Gandhi called on his fellow countrymen to "do or die" and demanded that British forces withdraw from India completely. More arrests followed.

On the world stage, Britain had been drained of resources. And the struggle for independence in India was stronger than ever. To add to the misfortunes of the British Empire, there was also an insurgency in their Balochistan colony, further depleting their resources. Despite the travesties it faced, the British refused to give in to the demands of the Indian leaders. The Quit India Movement was squashed on the basis of the notion that no independence could be granted during a war. The arrested leaders were kept in complete isolation with no news of the world reaching them. Gandhi, because of his depleting health resources, was released from prison in 1944. The other leaders would only be released much later. The gloomy burden of yet another failed movement was weighing down on many.

But around the same time, in 1945, the Labour Party was elected to power. Clement Attlee became the Prime Minister. Attlee had been a part of the Simon Commission back in the day and advocated India's right to self-governance. Finally, preparations were afoot for India to be free.

CHAPTER 8

THE CASUALTY OF PARTITION

The almost 200-year-old British-Indian connection was to be severed. On February 20th, 1947, Attlee made the announcement. The British would finally be leaving the country leaving the Indians to govern themselves all on their own. Attlee ordered Lord Mountbatten, India's last Viceroy, to draw up a plan for the transfer of power.

In May 1947, Mountbatten came up with what came to be known as the Dickie Bird Plan or the Balkan Plan. Here he suggested a constituent assembly that would be joined by the provinces that preferred it. However, Jawaharlal Nehru, an influential member of Congress, was strongly opposed to this idea. He was sure that this would lead to the fragmentation of the princely states into tiny states. Hence the name Balkan Plan stood for

Balkanization.

Mountbatten, thus, proposed another plan. This is known as the Mountbatten Plan and includes clauses for the formation of two states. Both states would have the right to formulate their own constitution and would have complete control over the matters of their respective states. The proposed plan was accepted by the Muslim League as well as Congress. There was one more provision that would impact these two nations as well as that of their citizens for years to come. The princely states were given the choice to stay independent or to join either of the two countries.

Two Nation Theory

By the time the Mountbatten Plan was announced, the news of partition was an accepted reality. Some stalwarts like Sardar Vallabh Bhai Patel had given in while some like Muhammad Ali Jinnah were rooting for it. Gandhi and Abdul Ghaffar Khan were the only two left in complete opposition to this plan. But what's interesting is that even that was not the beginning of this so-called Pakistan Movement.

Many people believe that the underlying cause for partition was the core differences in the lifestyles and culture of Hindus and

Muslims. People may think that there is so much history between these two, thanks to the Mughal emperors, that it would be impossible for them both to coexist. Well, there is some truth to that statement. There is indeed great history between the two. We have looked at it throughout this book. And we know that it's not all bad history. Sure, Mughal tyrants like Aurangzeb were cruel to their Hindu subjects, but when we look at Mughal history, he seems to be rather an exception than the rule. History is full of evidence that these two religions could have existed peacefully, even lovingly.

Therefore, one may say that it wasn't the fundamental differences between the two faiths that sowed the seeds of insecurity among the two but the British administration itself. After the Indian mutiny, the British carried the fear of protests almost until their rule ended. This is quite apparent in the divide and rule strategy employed by the administration under Lord Dufferin. Though he had permitted the formation of the Indian National Congress, he soon realized the power it could wield. As members started seeking more ways of participation Lord Dufferin steadily grew uncomfortable. He first tried approaching Congress directly requesting the members to keep their discussion limited to "non-political social reforms." When Congress refused he even reached out to the elite patrons of INC and tried to convince them to withdraw their patronage. When that didn't work he prohibited government officials from participating in the INC meetings.

Around the same time, he reached out to certain British loyalists in the Indian community. One of these people was Sir Syed Ahmad Khan. He was the same person who had pushed for Western, scientific education for Muslims in India. And thus began the speeches that would play upon people's insecurities. Syed Ahmad Khan was the first to speak about the two-nation theory in these speeches. The result was that by the early 1900s a section of the society firmly believed in the idea of a separate nation for Muslims. And thus was formed the All India Muslim League in 1906.

The All India Muslim League demanded that separate electorates be granted for Muslims where only the Muslims could be candidates for certain seats and only Muslims could vote for these. This demand was approved through Morley Minto Reforms or the Indian Council Act of 1909. This was the first outright communal administration passed by the government. This eventually led to a section of

Hindus feeling paranoid, and thus organizations like Rashtriya Swayamsevak Sangh (RSS) and the Akhil Bharatiya Hindu Mahasabha came into existence.

It's interesting to note that Muhammad Ali Jinnah who was a strong advocate of the need for a separate Muslim state in later years never supported these divisive moves. It's only later, possibly due to the cumulative effect of his life circumstances such as disagreements with Gandhi and the strong influence of Islamic extremists like poet Iqbal Khan, he eventually changed his mind. He wouldn't let the idea of Pakistan go even when Gandhi and Nehru offered him the position of Prime Minister of the independent state.

The Partition

The Indian Independence Act of 1947 received royal assent on July 8th, 1947 and it would be in effect from August 15th, 1947. This would be a joyous celebration if it wasn't marred by the pain and horror of Partition. About five weeks prior to the British departure from India, a lawyer, Sir Cyril Radcliffe, was hastily sent in. He arrived on July 8th, 1947, and was ordered to draw the line that would determine the fate of these two countries for a long time to come. For someone who had no understanding of the people or the place, this was an impossible task. Yet, Radcliffe drew a line, the "Bloody Line" as it is often called.

Dividing a multicultural nation like India on the basis of religion could not have been an easy task. States like Punjab and Bengal for instance had both massive Hindu and Muslim populations with neither in a clear majority. Another major problem was posed by the princely states which covered nearly 48% of the Indian territory (Pal, 2017). These could not be partitioned as they weren't under British occupation. So, they would be given the choice to stay independent or to join one of the two countries.

Ultimately, a bizarre line was drawn that seemed to travel through people's homes and hearts alike. For instance, the two holy sites of the Sikhs, some fifty-odd kilometers apart, were now in two different countries. Eastern and Western extremities of India were determined to be territories of Pakistan which formed Eastern Pakistan (later formed into a separate nation of Bangladesh) and Western Pakistan.

The partition was followed by a mass exodus as millions of Hindus, Muslims, and Sikhs were made to leave their homes and travel to the nation where they supposedly belonged. Riots ensued as children were slaughtered and women raped to prove the superiority of the perpetrators' religion, whatever it may be. The people of the two countries still feel the pain as memories come rushing and there are still families that live right across the border and have hardly seen each other.

The Republic of India

Partition had left a scar in India's freedom struggle. But, now it was time to build a nation from scratch. And Indians seemed ready for the challenges, of which there were many. Jawaharlal Nehru was nominated as the first Prime Minister of independent India. Primarily, there were millions of refugees who had come from Pakistan with neither homes and jobs nor any means of securing them. Next, the pockets of princely states had to be diplomatically managed because otherwise, they would create major administrative issues. Thanks to Sardar Vallabh Bhai Patel's diplomacy only three states were left to sign the instrument of accession—Jammu and Kashmir, Junagadh, and Hyderabad. But still, this was a crucial issue because of the strategic placement of these states. And lastly, a constitution had to be formed to ensure that the independence that people had fought for remained secure for ages to come.

But before Indian people could recover from the shock of partition, they had to face yet another catastrophe. On January 30th, 1948, Gandhi was shot as he was about to conduct one of his daily multifaith prayer meetings by a man called Nathuram Godse. Godse was a member of the right-wing organizations mentioned before—the Hindu Mahasabha and the Rashtriya Swayamsevak Sangh (RSS). He was vehemently opposed to Gandhi's ideals and believed that he had always engaged in appeasement politics. He feared that if Gandhi were to live, he would divide the country even further to appease the minorities. He was arrested and was given the death sentence. Regardless of whether people agreed with Gandhi or not, losing him was yet another blow to the already wounded people.

Regardless, there was no time to stop and Nehru put his best men to work. Sardar Vallabh Bhai Patel, a seasoned diplomat, and the Deputy Prime Minister, was given the task of integrating the remaining princely states into the federation of India. Junagadh and Hyderabad had joined the Indian state by 1948.

The situation with Kashmir proved to be tricky. Maharaja Hari Singh of Kashmir had also acceded his state to India on October 26th, 1947, a little after the Indian independence. But Pakistan claimed that their armies were in standstill agreement with the king, therefore making the accession instrument null and void. During this time, Lord Mountbatten was still the Viceroy and he accepted Hari Singh's accession but also mentioned that a referendum with the people of Kashmir would be conducted. However, the referendum never happened and Kashmir is still the bone of contention between the two countries. Multiple wars have been fought between the two countries for control over this strategically placed state.

The problem of the Constitution was also resolved as Nehru put that responsibility on the able shoulders of B. R. Ambedkar. Being from a socially oppressed caste and hailing from a humble background, Ambedkar was of the opinion that the Constitution had to be a tool for social reform if nothing else. He sought to base this all-important national document on equality and freedom. India was to be the largest democracy where people would have the right to vote for their representatives and thus play an indirect role in the functioning of the state. India became a republic on January 26th, 1950.

The last of the worries was the rehabilitation of the refugees. This concern would pose the toughest challenge yet. Refugees who had lost everything obviously didn't have a positive outlook towards the government. But Nehru and his bureaucrats were laying the plan for the future. The idea was to develop new hubs of development in unutilized regions. Central Province (present-day Chattisgarh, Madhya Pradesh, Maharashtra) seemed like a good option. To hasten this process, an agricultural revolution was also undertaken and many new loan schemes were introduced to help people rebuild their lives.

CONCLUSION
THE NEW INDIA

India, as a culture and as a nation, has had a colorful history. Over the centuries, it has been a melting pot of various traditions, heritages, and beliefs. Sure, it has been painful at times, and at times even bizarre, but it has survived all the storms and maybe even come out stronger. Partition is the unfortunate proof. But no one can deny that India emerged out of the ordeal successfully and has been a growing formidable economy on the world map.

But the journey since independence has not been easy. At the first elections in 1952, Nehru was re-elected as the Prime Minister, and also again in 1957 and 1962. He was a people's man after all. The developmental plans were divided into five-year plans. The first two five-year plans rightly focused on the development of agriculture and industries. This gave an impetus to rapid growth first of the rural sector and then of the urban sector. The states were also reorganized and the French and Portuguese colonies were also acquired through military offensive.

While India had positive global relations, it has had a murky history with its border neighbors. Immediately after independence, the Kashmir war was fought in 1947–48 which concluded in Pakistan occupying a part of

Kashmir, which is still called POK (Pakistan-

Occupied-Kashmir). Wars and ceasefires have continued in Kashmir all along, making it difficult for people to have a normal life. Nehru is often blamed for his approach with Pakistan as well as for the defeat of Indian forces by China in 1962.

For a long time, Congress had a great hold over the political scene in the country. India saw greats like Lal Bahadur Shastri, Morarji Desai, and so on assume positions of power. However, it started becoming apparent that the Nehru/Gandhi family was not willing to let go of its iron clasp over the political happenings.

Nehru's daughter Indira Gandhi was no doubt a formidable and loved leader. But she also turned out to be one who made the most controversial decisions including declaring a state of emergency. She was eventually assassinated by her Sikh bodyguards. As years passed by these dissatisfactions became prominent and the changing face of Indian politics resulted in a lowered appreciation for the policies of Congress. Eventually, many new parties emerged and the nation has proved to be one of the most vibrant democracies in the world.

As India entered into the 21st century, the tools and styles of politics have changed but what remains steadfast is the people's hope to elect something better. Regardless of the setbacks this nation has faced every now and then, it has surely emerged victorious. During the transfer of power from the British to the Indian state, many wondered if India was ready. Many speculated that the Indian democracy would be nothing but a disaster. But the truth is Indian democracy has only matured over the years. It doesn't mean there are no problems—there certainly are. The right-wing movement that is catching on across the world has also had its impact on India but it continues to evolve through these changes.

If you enjoyed reading this book and found it helpful, please leave a review on Amazon. It shall help us reach more curious minds with this brilliant story. May we all learn from stories and histories.

REFERENCES

Byju's. (2021, August 2). *How the Kalinga war changed Emperor Ashoka | Class 6 | Learn with Byju's.* YouTube. https://www.youtube.com/watch?v=b30KeI8zzeQ

Chandra, B., Mukherjee, M., Mukherjee, A., Mahajan, S., & Panikkar, K. N. (2003). *India's struggle for independence, 1857-1947.* Penguin.

Dabas, M. (2017, August 17). *Trending stories on Indian lifestyle, culture, relationships, food, travel, entertainment, news & new technology news.* Indiatimes. https://www.indiatimes.com/news/india/here-s-how-radcliff-line-was-drawn-on-this-day-and-lahore-could-not-become-a-part-of-india-328012.html

Dalrymple, W. (2015, June 22). *The mutual genocide of Indian Partition.* The New Yorker. https://www.newyorker.com/magazine/2015/06/29/the-great-divide-books-dalrymple

History's Histories. (2018). *India Gupta empire.* http://www.historyshistories.com/india-gupta-empire.html

Kapoor, R. (2021, August 14). *Build the refugee, build the state: Development & rehabilitation in post-partition india.* Refugee History. http://refugeehistory.org/blog/2017/8/12/build-the-refugee-build-the-state-development-rehabilitation-in-post-partition-india

Keay, J. (2011). *India: A history.* Crane Library At The University Of British Columbia.

Majumdar, R. C., Raychaudhuri, H. C., & Datta, K. (1974).

An advanced history of India. Delhi.

Mark, J. (2020, May 24). *Ashoka the Great*. World History Encyclopedia. https://www.worldhistory.org/Ashoka_the_Great/

National Geographic Society. (2020, August 20). *Mauryan empire*. National Geographic Society. https://www.nationalgeographic.org/encyclopedia/mauryan-empire/#:~:text=The%20Mauryan%20Empire%2C%20which%20formed

Pal, S. (2017, December 16). *The making of a nation: How Sardar Patel integrated 562 princely states*. The Better India. https://www.thebetterindia.com/124500/sardar-patel-vp-menon-integration-princely-states-india-independence/

Paul, S. (2021, March 17). *Yes, Gandhi did his utmost to save the lives of Bhagat Singh, Sukhdev and Rajguru, writes Sumit Paul*. Free Press Journal. https://www.freepressjournal.in/analysis/yes-gandhi-did-his-utmost-to-save-the-lives-of-bhagat-singh-sukhdev-and-rajguru-writes-sumit-paul

Pletcher, K. (2021, February 26). *Gandhi-Irwin Pact | Indian history*. Encyclopedia Britannica. https://www.britannica.com/event/Gandhi-Irwin-Pact

Rathee, D. (2021, August 15). *Partition 1947 / Why it happened? | India and Pakistan | Dhruv Rathee*. YouTube. https://www.youtube.com/watch?v=r2kKsjZPrVI

Study IQ Education. (2019, October 6). *Biography of Muhammad Ali Jinnah, Founder and first governor general of Pakistan*. YouTube. https://www.youtube.com/watch?v=NOKcSYZZwpg

Thapar, R. (2015). *The Penguin history of early India: from the origins to A.D.1300*. Penguin Books.

Yadav, A. K., & Chaudhary, S. (2021, April 14). *BR Ambedkar: Father of our Constitution and radical social thinker*. TheLeaflet. https://www.theleaflet.in/br-ambedkar-father-of-our-constitution-and-radical-social-thinker/

FREE BONUS FROM HBA: EBOOK BUNDLE

Greetings!

First of all, thank you for reading our books. As fellow passionate readers of History and Mythology, we aim to create the very best books for our readers.

Now, we invite you to join our VIP list. As a welcome gift, we offer the History & Mythology Ebook Bundle below for free. Plus you can be the first to receive new books and exclusives! Remember it's 100% free to join.

Simply scan the QR code down below to join.

OTHER BOOKS BY HISTORY BROUGHT ALIVE

Available now in Ebook, Paperback, Hardcover, and Audiobook in all regions.

Other books:

RECKONING
OF
POWER

SCANDINAVIAN
HISTORY

MYTHOLOGY
OF MESOPOTAMIA

For Kids:

HISTORY &
MYTHOLOGY
FOR KIDS
HISTORY BROUGHT ALIVE

GREEK
MYTHOLOGY
FOR KIDS
HISTORY BROUGHT ALIVE

EGYPTIAN
MYTHOLOGY
FOR KIDS
HISTORY BROUGHT ALIVE

MYTHOLOGY
FOR KIDS
HISTORY BROUGHT ALIVE

THE HISTORY OF
ENGLAND
FOR KIDS
HISTORY BROUGHT ALIVE

CELTIC
HISTORY
& MYTHOLOGY
FOR KIDS
Explore Timeless Tales, Characters,
History, & Legendary Stories from The Celts
HISTORY BROUGHT ALIVE

WORLD WAR 2
HISTORY
FOR KIDS
HISTORY BROUGHT ALIVE

NATIVE AMERICAN
HISTORY
FOR KIDS
HISTORY BROUGHT ALIVE

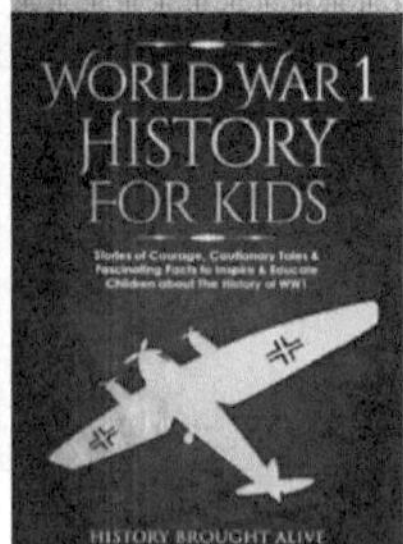
WORLD WAR 1
HISTORY
FOR KIDS
HISTORY BROUGHT ALIVE

THE HISTORY OF INDIA

We sincerely hope you enjoyed our new book ***"The History of India"***. We would greatly appreciate your feedback with an honest review at the place of purchase.

First and foremost, we are always looking to grow and improve as a team. It is reassuring to hear what works, as well as receive constructive feedback on what should improve. Second, starting out as an unknown author is exceedingly difficult, and Amazon reviews go a long way toward making the journey out of anonymity possible. Please take a few minutes to write an honest review.

Best regards,

History Brought Alive

http://historybroughtalive.com/

Made in United States
Troutdale, OR
05/20/2024